HOW GRANDPARENTS CAN HELP

—— WHEN ——

BAD THINGS HAPPEN

Lorene Hanley Duquin

Copyright © 2025 Lorene Duquin
All rights reserved.

Published by The Word Among Us Press
7115 Guilford Drive, Suite 100
Frederick, Maryland 21704
wau.org

29 28 27 26 25   1 2 3 4 5

ISBN: 978-1-59325-732-3
eISBN: 978-1-59325-733-0

Unless otherwise noted, Scripture texts in this work are taken from the Catholic Edition of the Revised Standard Version of the Bible, copyright © 1965, 1966 National Council of the Churches of Christ in the United States of America. Used by permission. All rights reserved worldwide.

Design by Rose Audette

No part of this publication may be reproduced, stored in a retrieval system, or transmitted in any form or by any means—electronic, mechanical, photocopy, recording, or any other—except for brief quotations in printed reviews, without the prior permission of the author and publisher.

Library of Congress Control Number: 2025940461

Contents

Introduction 5

Questions About What Happened 11

Questions About Yourself 23

Questions About Your Family 37

Questions About God 45

Questions About Other People 57

Questions About the Past 65

Questions About the Present 75

Questions About the Future 87

Afterword 95

INTRODUCTION

I recently participated in an online Faith Café meeting with members of the Catholic Grandparents Association from all over the world. We talked about bad things that happen in families. I was astounded at the outpouring from grandparents, who spoke about the difficulties they were experiencing and their concerns about how they could help their grandchildren.

Throughout our conversation, it occurred to me that before we can help our grandchildren with bad things that have happened, we have to come to grips with whatever happened to us. Just like a flight attendant would tell us that, in case of an emergency, we should put on our own oxygen mask before we try to help others, so we have to find our own ways to cope with what happened before we can assist our grandchildren.

This is not easy. It doesn't matter if the bad thing is big or small; when it happens, it can feel overwhelming. Adding to our angst might be the feeling that we are the only family who has ever experienced something like this—even though we know this is not true.

> "Ask, and it will be given you; seek, and you will find; knock, and it will be opened to you. For everyone who asks receives, and he who seeks finds, and to him who knocks it will be opened."
>
> —Matthew 7:7-8

I am a wife, mother, grandmother, and the matriarch of my extended family. During my lifetime, a lot of good things have happened. But my family has also experienced deaths, divorces, cancer diagnoses, serious illnesses, accidents, addictions, suicide attempts, house fires, and hurricanes. I have family members who lost their faith. I have seen family relationships end in anger. I have felt deep disappointment over choices loved ones have made.

While I was researching for this book, a number of grandparents shared their experiences with me. They spoke about family situations involving mental illness, disabilities, eating disorders, criminal behavior, lifestyle choices, nontraditional family situations, unplanned pregnancies, abortions, financial difficulties, incarceration, abuse, and betrayals. They also offered their own stories, insights, and advice, which I have included in this book anonymously to protect their privacy.

You probably are not reading this today unless something bad has happened in your family. The purpose of this book is not to dwell on the bad things that happen but, rather, to focus on how we as grandparents can come to grips with whatever bad thing happened. At the end of each section, there are practical suggestions on how we can help our grandchildren.

Throughout the book we explore some of the tough questions that arise in our hearts, minds, and souls when we encounter difficulties and disappointments. Wrestling with questions is never easy. Some of the questions in this book may be more challenging than others. You may find yourself skipping over some questions entirely. You may find yourself struggling with other questions that are not addressed.

Please don't be discouraged if you are unable to find immediate answers to your questions. When bad things happen, it can feel as if you have been plunged into total darkness with no sense of direction. This is when your Catholic faith will come into play. I have also included a number of prayers that you may find helpful.

Research shows that people with strong spiritual beliefs are better able to weather the storms in life. Sometimes we just need to stand still until the worst of the storm passes and wait for God to provide us with enough light to move forward one step at a time.

Eventually we emerge from the darkness. Our lives never go back to the way they were before, but we gain new insights, new understandings, new ways of coping, and new feelings of hope. It is my prayer that this little book will help you to weather whatever storm is battering you and give you the wisdom and the strength to help your grandchildren.

INTRODUCTION

PRAY ABOUT IT

Here is a powerful prayer that we can rely on when bad things happen:

> Every day I need you, Lord, but today especially, I need some extra strength to face whatever is to come. This day, more than any other day, I need to feel you near me to strengthen my courage and to overcome any fear. By myself I cannot meet the challenge of the hour. We are frail human creatures and we need a higher power to sustain us in all that life may bring. And so, dear Lord, hold my trembling hand. Be with me, Lord, this day and stretch out your powerful arm to help me. May your love be upon me as I place all my hope in you. Amen.[1]

QUESTIONS FOR REFLECTION AND DISCUSSION

1. What happened that caused you to pick up this book?
2. What are your greatest concerns?
3. What are some of the questions you would like to have answered?

---

[1] Commonly attributed to Pope St. John XXIII.

CHAPTER ONE

QUESTIONS ABOUT WHAT HAPPENED

Did This Really Happen?

It is not unusual to find ourselves in a state of shock and denial when something bad happens. We may find ourselves thinking it is just a bad dream and everything will go back to normal in a few days. We may feel numb. We may find ourselves saying, "I can't believe this happened." Or we may tell ourselves it must be a mistake.

One grandmother recalled that for several hours after she learned that her son and grandson had died in an automobile accident, she just stared at a clock and watched the second hand move around second by second.

Another grandmother admitted she simply could not believe it when her son told her he was getting a divorce.

A grandfather refused to accept that his teenage granddaughter had been arrested for shoplifting.

Another grandfather could not believe his teenage grandson had attempted suicide.

These feelings of shock and disbelief insulate us from the harsh reality for a while. Eventually the shock wears off and denial is no longer possible. The situation becomes more real, and our prayer may take on a tone of bargaining: "Lord, if you can make this go away, I will go to Mass every day!"

After a while, the reality of what happened settles into our minds and hearts. It takes time.

Why? Why? Why?

When bad things happen, we may find ourselves asking "why" questions: Why now? Why did it happen to our family? Why did it happen this way?

Asking "Why?" is our attempt to make sense out of something we can't comprehend. We assume that if we knew the reason, the reality of what happened might be easier to accept. The problem is that there may not be an answer. Other people's attempts to answer our "why" questions usually do not comfort or satisfy us.

Sometimes "Why?" is not really a question but rather a cry of protest, helplessness, or pain.

"I really struggled with why my wife died," one grandfather admitted. "I always thought I would go first. I never got an answer, but my faith helped me get through it. It helped me believe that death is not the end. I will see my wife again."

How Did This Happen?

When something bad happens, our world can feel as if it's spinning out of control, and we begin to wonder how it happened. Knowing how a bad thing happened can give us something concrete to point to: "This happened because . . ." Knowing how the bad thing happened can also give us a place to lay blame: someone did something wrong. Someone was careless. Someone acted without thinking. Someone got sick. Someone took a risk. Someone was influenced in a bad way and made a bad decision.

Blame may answer *how* something happened, but it doesn't change anything. Blame doesn't help us find a solution to the problem. Blame doesn't make us feel better. In fact, blaming someone for what happened often makes us feel worse because it stirs up negative emotions such as anger, resentment, or hatred.

Blame tends to be judgmental and accusatory. It pushes away the people we are blaming and can leave us feeling isolated and upset. When a person we are blaming is someone we love, we run the risk of destroying the relationship. Even if the person is not someone we care about, blame can have consequences.

One grandmother admitted that she placed all the blame on her daughter-in-law for her son's divorce, but when the daughter-in-law got custody of the children, the grandmother began to see that it didn't matter who was at fault. What mattered was maintaining a relationship with the daughter-in-law who controlled access to her grandchildren.

> He heals the brokenhearted, and binds up their wounds.
>
> —Psalm 147:3

If you find yourself starting to blame someone for what happened, ask God to help you move beyond blame. Ask for the ability to recognize that we all make mistakes. Ask for humility to admit that you do not know the full story. Ask for wisdom to see that we all need compassion and understanding. Ask for the courage to forgive.

What If No One Is to Blame?

Sometimes the bad thing that happened was an accident, a fluke of nature, a twist of fate, or simply someone being in the wrong place at the wrong time. You may feel anger or outrage at the unfairness of what happened. You may feel that you and your family members are innocent victims.

"Our home was destroyed in a tornado," one grandparent explained. "Our neighbor's house was fine. We didn't have anyone to blame except Mother Nature."

It's OK to blame Mother Nature or bad luck for what happened. But if you remain focused on blame, you will delay your own healing process. Constantly thinking and talking about blame is like continually ripping the scab off a wound.

"I had to keep telling myself that it didn't matter who was to blame," one grandfather admitted. "What happened was over and done. I reached a point where I didn't want to talk about blame anymore. I wanted to move on."

What If?

When something bad happens, we may wonder whether we could have done something to prevent it. We may wonder whether something we did in the past caused what happened. We may ask: Did I do enough? Did I do too much? What if I had done this? What if I hadn't done that? Is there something else I should have done?

Most people come to see that what they agonize about wouldn't have made any difference. One grandmother blamed herself for not noticing her grandson's symptoms, but the cancer had already spread too far for a cure. A grandfather refused to let his granddaughter borrow his car, and she got into an accident with another teenager's car. Both of these grandparents had no way of seeing into the future. They are not responsible for what happened.

Sometimes, however, we recognize that we did play a role in what happened, and it unleashes feelings of guilt and remorse. The Sacrament of Reconciliation can be a tremendous help to people struggling with "what if" questions. Whether you are blaming yourself or someone else, a priest can help you sort through some of the emotional turmoil that you feel. He can bring you God's healing forgiveness and help you to forgive yourself and other people.

Why Can't I Stop Thinking About This?

When bad things happen, we may find ourselves replaying the incidents over and over in our minds. These repetitive thoughts shatter our concentration, disturb our sleep, and increase our anxiety. To break the cycle, we need to make conscious efforts to distract ourselves. It helps to keep telling ourselves, "I am not going to think about this now."

It also helps if we can force ourselves to move in a different direction. Start a new project, volunteer to help someone else, go for a nature walk, join a prayer group, or keep busy with people or activities that will keep your mind off of what happened.

"The more isolated I become, the harder it is for me to control my thoughts," one grandmother admitted. "I have to make a conscious effort to reach out to friends when I find my imagination running wild."

If you can't stem the repetitive thoughts on your own and you feel yourself sinking into depression, it's time to seek professional help.

Could It Happen Again?

It is not unusual to worry about whether things will get worse in the future. We may worry about whether new difficulties will unfold. We may worry that the same bad thing will happen again.

Whenever we worry about the future, we have to remind ourselves that God is with us in the present moment. God's grace sustains us right now. If we allow ourselves to become distracted about what might happen in the future, we don't notice the ways in which God's healing love is with us right now. We miss the inspirations of the Holy Spirit that are guiding us.

"I was paralyzed with fear about what might happen next," one grandmother admitted. "A priest finally told me that my fear was lack of faith. He suggested that we pray together. He put his hands on my head, and I felt a calm presence come over me. The priest told me it was God's presence. I never felt that presence again, but I know it was real, and it took away my fear of the future."

HOW TO HELP YOUR GRANDCHILDREN

Here are some ways to help your grandchildren in the immediate aftermath of something bad that has happened:

1. Realize that your grandchildren may be experiencing the same shock and denial that you feel. Don't try to force a conversation. Just be present to them. Admit to them that you are also struggling with what happened.

2. If your grandchildren ask "Why?" admit that you have the same questions and that you don't have answers. Tell them that sometimes there are no answers.

3. If your grandchildren want to know how it happened, you may or may not be able to give them a detailed explanation. Promise that you will always tell them the truth. Avoid blame at all costs. Encourage them to let go of blame, which only makes everything worse.

4. If your grandchildren wonder if they caused their parents' divorce or the death of a family member, assure them it was not their fault. If they were responsible for whatever bad thing happened, you can help by listening, by emphasizing that you will always love them, and by encouraging their parents to get professional help for them if needed.

5. If your grandchildren are overly obsessed with what happened, try to plan activities or adventures that will break their negative thought patterns. Tell them that you will never abandon them. Let them know that you are willing to walk with them through this troubling time.

6. Pray for your grandchildren, and offer to pray with them.

PRAY ABOUT IT

Take some time to prayerfully reflect on the words of St. Francis de Sales:

> Be at peace.
>
> Do not look forward in fear to the changes of life;
>
> rather look to them with full hope as they arise.
>
> God, whose very own you are, will deliver you safely from out of them.
>
> He has kept you hitherto, and He will lead you safely through all things;
>
> and when you cannot stand it, God will bury you in his arms.
>
> Do not fear what may happen tomorrow;
>
> the same everlasting Father who cares for you today will take care of you then and every day.
>
> He will either shield you from suffering, or give you unfailing strength to bear it.
>
> Be at peace, and put aside all anxious thoughts and imagination.[2]

---

[2] "The Prayer of St. Francis de Sales," Sisters of the Divine Savior, https://www.sistersofthedivinesavior.org/pray_archive/the-prayer-of-st-francis-de-sales.

QUESTIONS FOR REFLECTION AND DISCUSSION

1. Do you still have a hard time believing that this bad thing happened?

2. In what ways have you wrestled with "why" and "what if" questions?

3. How have you dealt with repetitive thoughts?

4. How have you been able to reach out to your grandchildren?

CHAPTER TWO

QUESTIONS ABOUT YOURSELF

Why Do I Feel like This?

When bad things happen, we are thrust into a grieving process. Grief is most commonly associated with the death of a loved one. But we grieve other losses, such as the death of relationships when family members divorce or become estranged. We grieve the death of our dreams when our children or grandchildren make choices that conflict with our beliefs or values. We grieve when accidents or natural disasters damage or destroy homes or possessions. We grieve when serious illness or disability threatens our lives or disrupts our ability to do the things we want to do. We grieve whenever bad things happen.

Grief is the process by which healing takes place after we suffer a loss. You may be familiar with the five stages of

"Many of us spend our whole lives running from feeling with the mistaken belief that we cannot bear the pain. But you have already borne the pain. What you have not done is feel all that you are beyond the pain."

—Unknown Author

grief that focus on feelings: shock, denial, anger, sadness, and acceptance. Some people go through the stages in order, while others jump from one stage to another. You can also experience several stages at the same time.

It helps to remind yourself that the feelings associated with grief ebb and flow at different levels of intensity. One day you may feel calm and the next day you may be devasted. There is no timetable for how long the grieving process lasts. Eventually the raw pain subsides, and you begin to accept that life goes on—not necessarily in the way you had hoped, but in new ways that offer new opportunities for faith, hope, and love.

"One morning I woke up and I knew that I needed to accept what was happening, even though it was not what I wanted," one grandparent said. "The situation didn't change, but I knew I was going to be able to get through this."

Can I Avoid the Grieving Process?

You can try to sidestep the pain of grief by bottling it up inside, but it will only make the process longer and more difficult. Suppressed feelings do not go away. They fester inside of us, and eventually the painful feelings will resurface. Think of how difficult it would be to hold a log underwater for an extended period of time. It would demand a lot of your attention and energy to keep that log submerged. At some point, usually when you are distracted by something else, you will forget to hold the log down, and it will pop up to the surface.

Some people try to deaden the pain of grief with alcohol, pills, drugs, food, or other compulsive behaviors. Sometimes the smoldering grief explodes in angry outbursts over completely unrelated things. There is an old saying that you can't go around grief, over it, or under it; you have to go *through* it.

How Can I Work Through This?

Start by acknowledging what you feel—anger, guilt, frustration, disappointment, hurt, shame, fear, envy, hate. It is possible to feel several strong emotions at the same time. For example, on the surface you may feel angry, but other emotions, such as sadness, fear, or worry, may be fueling the anger.

Look for a safe person with whom you can talk openly and honestly. Find someone who will listen, who doesn't tell you what to say or do, and who lets you express your feelings. It is only when you begin to let your feelings out that you can begin to heal.

One grandfather admitted that feelings of anger and deep disappointment kept rising inside him after he learned his grandson had been arrested for shoplifting.

A grandmother admitted she felt consumed by sadness and deep feelings of loneliness after her grandchildren moved three thousand miles away.

Talking about how you feel is not an instant cure, but it is a crucial first step. Remind yourself it is OK to feel emotional when something bad happens. Emotions are a gift from God that are an important part of being human. Emotions help us to understand ourselves, connect with other people, and relate to the world around us. We can experience both positive and negative feelings when something bad happens. Think about how you've felt at a funeral of a loved one when you were sad about the death, but you could also laugh when people told funny stories about the person who died.

God also gifted us with an intellect that allows us to think about how we are feeling, and a free will that allows us to choose what we will say or do in response. How we react to our feelings of grief is an important part of working through the grieving process.

"After my wife died, it wasn't the big holidays that were the hardest for me," one grandfather admitted. "It was the everyday things like making coffee for just me in the morning. I decided to stop making my own coffee and go to a coffee shop instead. It was a good decision. I met some people who encouraged me to join them every morning. They don't mind if I talk about my wife. They have become my new friends."

Grieving is not easy. Be patient with yourself. Expect that some days will be harder than others. Ask God for the wisdom and courage to deal with your painful emotions in a positive way. Some things will always hurt, but the sharpness of the pain will lessen, and you will regain a sense of peace.

Allow these words from the Book of Isaiah to penetrate the deepest part of yourself:

When you pass through waters I will be with you;
    and through the rivers, they shall not overwhelm you;
when you walk through fire you shall not be burned,
    and the flame shall not consume you.
For I and the Lord your God,
    the Holy One of Israel, your Savior.

—Isaiah 43:2-3

Why Do I Feel So Tired?

During troubling times, your body releases stress hormones into your system. These hormones are primitive responses that prepare your body to deal with danger by fighting or fleeing. Your physical response to these hormones can include a racing heart, tightness in the chest, and changes in your breathing patterns that can range from hyperventilating to holding your breath.

When your body recognizes there is no physical threat looming, it lowers the stress hormones, which can make you feel exhausted. Broken sleep patterns can add to your lack of energy and fatigue.

Acknowledging that you are under a great deal of stress is the first step in dealing with it. Other stress-reduction techniques include:

- Setting aside time several times each day to clear your mind and relax your muscles. Some people use this time to repeat a simple prayer such as, "Lord, have mercy," or, "Jesus help me."

- Eating well-balanced meals, taking daily vitamins, and drinking plenty of water.

- Staying away from junk food, sugary drinks, caffeine, and alcohol.

- Exercising for twenty to thirty minutes each day—even if it is just walking around the house.

♦ Consulting your physician if you are losing too much weight, neglecting personal hygiene, ignoring the necessary activities of daily life, or relying on over-the-counter or prescription drugs to ease your anxiety.

Why Can't I Stop Crying?

Crying is an important part of the healing process. Studies have shown that an enzyme in the tears of a grieving person allows their body to release the toxins associated with stress.

Crying is also an emotional release. It helps you release the pain inside of you.

After the death of her grandson, one grandmother recalled walking into a grocery store and bursting into tears when she saw a display of watermelons. "It was my grandson's favorite fruit, and I could not stop crying. I had to go back out to the car."

"I was always told that strong men don't cry," one grandfather admitted. "But after my wife died, I cried a lot. The tears would come, and I couldn't stop them."

When something bad happens, you may find yourself crying when you least expect it. A song, a photo, a scent, or even the face of a complete stranger may trigger your tears. You may feel embarrassed if you start to cry in public. Simply excuse yourself and allow yourself to cry. As time goes on, these kinds of crying episodes will become less frequent and not as intense.

You can transform your tears into a prayer with the words of Psalm 102 (see page 32).

How Do I Deal with Feelings of Guilt and Shame?

Guilt and shame can arise when our children or grandchildren act in ways that conflict with what we believe is right or wrong. When we experience guilt, we accuse ourselves of doing something that caused what happened or failing to do something that could have prevented it: "I did a bad thing." When we experience shame, we accuse ourselves of being bad because of what happened: "I am a bad person."

It is not unusual for grandparents to experience feelings of guilt or shame because children or grandchildren make what the grandparents consider immoral lifestyle choices. Addictions, abortions, sexual orientation, severed relationships, breaking the law, and forsaking their Catholic faith are a few examples.

"It goes against everything I was raised to believe," one grandfather lamented. "But there is nothing I can do about it."

"I don't agree with the choices some of my grandchildren are making," a grandmother admitted. "I don't understand how all of this became accepted today. I love them, but I am so ashamed of them."

The first step in dealing with guilt and shame is to ask ourselves whether we played a role in what happened. If the answer is yes, the Sacrament of Reconciliation can help us accept God's forgiveness and forgive ourselves.

Do not hide thy face from me
 in the day of my distress!
Incline thy ear to me;
 answer me speedily in the day when I call!

—Psalm 102:2

In most cases, however, we cannot blame ourselves for decisions made by our adult children and grandchildren. There has been a huge cultural shift over the past fifty years that has influenced the life choices people make. Loving a child or a grandchild does not mean loving everything they say or do. Sometimes we just have to hold our family members in prayer, accept that we are not going to change them, and trust in the unconditional love and mercy of God.

Why Do I Feel So Hopeless?

It is normal for people to feel sad and upset when something bad happens. These feelings are different than the feelings of clinical depression, which stifle your ability to experience brief moments of pleasure, find meaning in your life, take on the functions of daily life, or look to the future with glimmers of hope. If you recognize these kinds of hopelessness in yourself or someone else in your family, it is time to seek professional help.

HOW TO HELP YOUR GRANDCHILDREN

Your grandchildren are probably going through all of the things you are experiencing. Here are some things you can do to help them:

1. Admit that you are grieving after what happened. Explain to them that grief is a normal process, and share the stages of grief and the strong emotions you are experiencing.

2. Encourage them to talk about how they feel physically and emotionally.

3. Assure them that it is OK to cry. Cry together.

4. Invite them to go for walks. Encourage them to stay hydrated. Avoid the temptation to feed them junk food. Offer healthy meals, fruits, and vegetables.

5. Listen if they are struggling with guilt or shame over something their parents or other family members did. Invite them to pray with you for the healing of the family.

6. Watch for signs that your grandchild is emotionally unstable or depressed. Be concerned if you see signs of hopelessness, inability to laugh or experience enjoyment, changes in eating or sleeping patterns, increased anxiety, or loss of interest in life. Your grandchild may need professional help.

PRAY ABOUT IT

Take some time to reflect on this powerful prayer from St. Ignatius of Loyola:

> O Christ Jesus
>
> When all is darkness,
>
> And we feel our weakness and helplessness,
>
> Give us the sense of Your Presence,
>
> Your Love and Your Strength.
>
> Help us to have perfect trust,
>
> In your protecting love,
>
> And strengthening power,
>
> So that nothing may frighten or worry us,
>
> For, living close to You,
>
> We shall see Your Hand,
>
> Your Purpose, Your Will through all things.[3]

---

[3] St. Ignatius of Loyola, "Ignatian Prayers," Xavier University, https://www.xavier.edu/jesuitresource/online-resources/prayer-index/ignatian-prayers.

QUESTIONS FOR REFLECTION AND DISCUSSION

1. In what ways are you grieving the bad thing that happened?

2. What physical symptoms have you experienced?

3. How do you deal with feelings of guilt or shame?

4. How have you reached out to your grandchildren?

CHAPTER THREE

QUESTIONS ABOUT YOUR FAMILY

Are They OK?

Checking up with family members on a regular basis to make sure they are OK is important—even if you live far away. Some family members may want to talk. Others may retreat into silence. Some may want to be with you. Others may want to be alone. No matter their preference, it's important to keep the lines of communication open.

One grandmother said texting "Thinking of you!" or "How are you doing today?" or "Is there anything I can do for you?" was the best way to communicate with her adult children and grandchildren during a difficult time.

What If They Refuse to Talk About It?

Be careful that you don't have expectations that other family members are unable or unwilling to meet. If they don't want to talk, let them be. The best thing you can do is love them unconditionally and be present if or when they decide to talk.

Should I Admit to My Children and Grandchildren That I Am Struggling with This?

Admitting that you are struggling shows your children and grandchildren that you are seeking ways to cope with what happened. It gives them permission to talk about how they are coping. It provides the opportunity for family members to say, "I am feeling the same way."

"Healing started to take place when my husband and I started to share how we felt about what happened," one grandmother admitted. "We never pressured anyone. We just let them know that we were suffering too."

Another grandmother reached out to family members by letting them know what she was doing to cope. She would say, "I am feeling really stressed, so I'm going to take a walk," or, "I am feeling really sad, so I'm going to pray the Rosary." She was delighted when her grandchildren began to ask if they could join in what she was doing to cope with the bad thing that happened.

Should I Offer My Opinion or Advice?

Unless a family member asks for your opinion or advice, it is usually best to say nothing. Inserting yourself into the family dynamic at a difficult time can create unneeded tension.

One grandfather admitted that when he has an observation about something that is happening in the family, he talks about it with his wife. "Sometimes you just have to wait for them to come to you—even if they make mistakes in the meantime that you could have helped them avoid," he said.

"I open the door by saying, 'Do you want to know what I think?'" another grandparent explained. "It's all about mutual respect. I don't want them to tell me what to do, so I won't tell them what I think they should do unless they ask."

What If My Family Members Don't Want My Help?

Family members will deal with what happened in their own ways. Some may turn to other family members or friends for support. You can't help someone who does not want your help. Sometimes we simply have to accept whatever family members say or do. The painful reality is that we don't have the ability to change other people. We can only change ourselves.

"I was surprised which family members rallied and which ones retreated into silence," one grandmother admitted. "As much as I wanted everyone to come together, I realized that I had to respect that each family member had his or her own way of dealing with this."

> Above all hold unfailing your love for one another, since love covers a multitude of sins.
>
> —1 Peter 4:8

What If They Threaten to Cut Me Off?

Severed relationships do not make life easier for anyone when families are in turmoil. If your children threaten to cut you off from themselves or your grandchildren, try to understand the reason for this threat. If the threat is a reaction to something you said or did—no matter if you were right or wrong—it may be best to extend an olive branch.

One grandfather was shocked when his wife wrote letters of apology to their ex-daughter-in-law after a bitter divorce. "You didn't do anything wrong!" he insisted. But the grandmother explained that she was trying to keep the lines of communication open because the daughter-in-law had custody of the children. "My wife's strategy worked," the grandfather said. "Our ex-daughter-in-law did not cut us off from our grandchildren."

Why Do I Feel as If All of This Is Killing Me?

It's not unusual for grandparents to become emotionally and physically depleted when trying to help family members through a crisis. Helping others is important, but your health and well-being are also important. If you begin to experience physical signs such as exhaustion, headaches, stomach or intestinal issues, insomnia, and anxiety, you need to talk to your doctor. You may still be able to help family members, but you need to prioritize your own health.

HOW TO HELP YOUR GRANDCHILDREN

The best thing grandparents can do during difficult times is to become a safe port in the storm.

1. Let your grandchildren know that they can speak freely and ask questions. Answer questions honestly, and explain that sometimes there is no answer. Assure them that you will not share what they tell you with anyone else.

2. Encourage younger grandchildren to express their feelings by drawing pictures or engaging in imaginative play. Allow them to cling to you and to cry. Read books together. Take them to a playground or go on an adventure walk. Be a calming presence in their lives.

3. With older children and teenagers, the best thing you can do is listen. You can share your feelings. You can allow them to express their emotions without trying to stifle or disrespect their feelings. You can assure them that good feelings will return.

4. You can pray for your grandchildren no matter their age. You can also offer to pray with them by saying something as simple as, "Let's ask the Lord to help us," "Let's ask the Holy Spirit to guide us through this," or, "Let's pray an Our Father or a Hail Mary together."

PRAY ABOUT IT

Take some time to reflect on the Serenity Prayer, which offers profound guidance for dealing with difficult family situations.

> God, grant me the serenity
>
> to accept the things I cannot change,
>
> courage to change the things I can,
>
> and wisdom to know the difference.[4]

QUESTIONS FOR REFLECTION AND DISCUSSION

1. What is your greatest concern about your family members during this difficult time?

2. How are your family members dealing with what happened?

3. How will you recognize that you are becoming emotionally depleted and exhausted?

4. In what ways have you helped your grandchildren?

---

[4] Reinhold Niebuhr, "Serenity Prayer," Alcoholics Anonymous, https://www.aa.org/sites/default/files/literature/assets/smf-141_en.pdf.

CHAPTER FOUR

QUESTIONS ABOUT GOD

Why Didn't God Stop This from Happening?

We may wonder why a loving, merciful, all-powerful God could allow this bad thing to happen. We may feel angry at God. We may wonder if we can trust God. We may wonder if God has abandoned us. We may be tempted to think what happened was some kind of divine punishment.

If we read the Book of Job in the Old Testament, we see that Job did nothing wrong. He didn't understand why God allowed bad things to happen to him. Job had a lot of questions. Like Job, we may cry out, "Let the Almighty answer me!" (31:35). But God didn't answer Job's questions. Instead, God asked questions that brought Job to a deeper level of understanding.

In the end, Job grew closer to God and realized that God had never abandoned him. God remained close to Job as he struggled with the mystery of why bad things happen; and even though God didn't answer Job's questions directly, God graced Job with his presence.

God doesn't abandon us either. God stays with us as we struggle—even if we are so troubled that we don't realize God is accompanying us. We may not recognize God's presence or how God helped us until much later when we look back and reflect on what happened.

Why Is Prayer So Difficult?

It's not unusual for people to find no comfort or consolation in prayer when bad things happen. Some people find it hard to turn to God as a source of strength when they blame God for allowing something bad to happen. Or they try to hide their true feelings from God because they are afraid God will get angry at them for being angry. Some people believe that if you are good, God will take care of you, and if you are bad, God will punish you.

But that's not how God deals with us. There is no answer to why innocent people suffer or why suffering is not equally distributed. Bad things can happen with no reason as to who deserves them and who doesn't.

Asking God these kinds of painful questions is a good way to pray when something bad happens. Simply pour out your heartache, your fears, your doubts, and your sorrow.

One grandmother admitted that the prayers she had relied on since childhood seemed empty after an accident left her grandchild permanently disabled. A priest suggested that she tell God how she feels. "Don't hold anything back," he advised. "Some of the best prayer happens when we open ourselves to God in this way."

But prayer isn't always talking to God. Sometimes prayer is listening. In our darkest moments, God whispers to us, "I am here," but we may be so absorbed in our pain that we don't hear him. Some people find it helpful to set aside a quiet time each day for listening. Simply clear your mind and sit quietly for several minutes, slowly repeating the name "Jesus." If distractions arise, clear your mind again and keep saying "Jesus" until a calm presence comes over you.

Another simple way to pray when going through a difficult time is to turn your breathing into a prayer. Close your eyes, take a deep breath, and imagine you are breathing in God's love. Then breathe out whatever negative feeling is inside you. Sit quietly for a few minutes, breathing in God's love and breathing out painful feelings. Imagine that God's love is flowing into every part of your being to calm you, to heal you, and to give you strength. You can do the breathing prayer at any time and in any place, and no one—except God and you—will know that you are praying.

Prayer brings us closer to God—even when it feels difficult. The more we turn to God in prayer, the more prayer changes us. We begin to recognize God's presence. We begin to believe that no matter what is happening in our lives, God is with us.

"When you come before the Lord, talk to him if you can; if you can't, just stay there, let yourself be seen, and don't try too hard to do anything else."
—St. Francis de Sales[5]

---

[5] Commonly attributed to St. Francis de Sales.

Is It Wrong to Feel Angry at God?

Anger is a natural response to something we perceive as an injustice. When bad things happen, we may feel hurt and deeply wounded, but on some level, we tell ourselves it is wrong to feel angry at God. This is simply not true. It's OK to say to God, "I'm angry because this person is sick," "I'm angry because this person died," "I'm angry because this bad thing happened," or, "I'm angry because it feels as if my family is falling apart."

Telling God how angry you feel is a powerful form of prayer because you are speaking honestly from the depths of yourself. God won't get angry at you for being angry. God doesn't retaliate. God sees your pain. God loves you no matter how you feel.

"A priest told me that when I'm angry at God, to keep fighting with him," one grandmother admitted. "It was good advice. I eventually began to let go of the anger. My family situation hadn't changed, but I began to feel calmer."

"Let us ask Our Lord to be with us in our moments of temptation. We must not be afraid because God loves us and will not fail to help us."

—St. Teresa of Calcutta[6]

---

[6] Commonly attributed to St. Teresa of Calcutta.

What Does God Want Me to Do?

When bad things happen, we are often faced with decisions to be made. The process of figuring out what God wants us to do can be a major concern. Sometimes the answer is painfully obvious: we know precisely what God wants us to do, and we may or may not want to do it.

In most cases, however, God's will for us is not crystal clear. We may feel as if we are being pulled in two directions. We may want to run away from the pain in our lives, but we may feel as if God is asking us to walk through this pain. We may want to avoid certain people, but we may feel that God is asking us to reach out. We may want to isolate ourselves, but we may feel that God is urging us to engage.

You can be sure that God is prompting you if you are being guided toward what is good. God never leads us toward what is hurtful, sinful, or wrong. Unfortunately, when bad things happen, we are often tempted to do something we should not.

What Are Some of the Temptations People Face When Bad Things Happen?

Many grandparents admitted they were bombarded with temptations during difficult times. Here are some of the struggles they faced:

- The temptation toward envy when they started to compare their lives with other people.

- The temptation toward hatred and revenge when they were unable to forgive people who had hurt them.

- The temptation to self-pity when they began to feel sorry for themselves.
- The temptation toward irritability when their frustration over what happened caused them to be unkind to others.
- The temptation to eavesdrop when they felt as if they were being excluded from conversations.
- The temptation toward pride when they refused to acknowledge that they needed help.
- The temptation to slip into negative thought patterns that led to criticism of themselves and others.
- The temptation to hold on to resentment.
- The temptation to turn away from God and stop praying.
- The temptation to despair when self-pity erodes faith and hope.

Why Am I Constantly Tempted to Seek Revenge for What Happened? I Pray for Help, But God Doesn't Stop These Horrible Thoughts.

God doesn't cause temptations, but he does allow them to happen. All the great saints had to overcome temptations. Temptations can strengthen our will, increase our faith, and help us recognize our need for God.

> St. Paul assures us, "God is faithful, and he will not let you be tempted beyond your strength, but with the temptation will also provide the way of escape, that you may be able to endure it" (1 Corinthians 10:13).

The best response when temptations arise is an immediate, "No!" The longer we allow temptations to linger, the more difficult they are to reject. Telling someone about our temptations moves them to the outside of ourselves and diminishes their power. Prayer is also good protection against temptations. A simple Our Father invites God to "deliver us from evil." Some people simply pray, "Jesus, have mercy on me," or, "Mother Mary, pray for me."

HOW TO HELP YOUR GRANDCHILDREN

You are in a unique position to help your grandchildren if they are struggling with God in the aftermath of what happened. Here are some suggestions:

1. Talk to them about free will and why God allows bad things to happen. Admit that it is a difficult concept to grasp when something bad is happening. Assure them that good things will happen again.

2. Assure them that it is OK to feel angry at God because of what happened and that even when they are angry, God still loves them. Share with them how you tell God when you are angry.

3. Talk to them about what you believe God wants you to do in the midst of this crisis. Tell them God always wants us to seek what is good.

4. Warn them that temptations to do something bad often arise during difficult times. Share how you overcome temptations. Talk about why revenge is never acceptable.

PRAY ABOUT IT

This powerful prayer invokes the help of St. Michael the Archangel when faced with temptations.

> St. Michael the Archangel, defend us in battle.
>
> Be our protection against the wickedness and snares of the devil.
>
> May God rebuke him, we humbly pray;
>
> and do Thou, O Prince of the Heavenly Host, by the Power of God,
>
> cast into hell Satan and all the evil spirits
>
> who prowl through the world seeking the ruin of souls. Amen.[7]

QUESTIONS FOR REFLECTION AND DISCUSSION

1. How has this difficult time affected your relationship with God?
2. How do you pray?
3. What temptations have you struggled with?
4. In what ways have you helped your grandchildren?

---

[7] Pope Leo XIII, "St. Michael the Archangel Prayer," The Catholic Company, https://www.catholiccompany.com/st-michael-the-archangel-prayer/.

CHAPTER FIVE

QUESTIONS ABOUT OTHER PEOPLE

Why Do I Feel So Uncomfortable Around Other People?

Maybe you've wondered if people at church are staring at you. Maybe you've walked into a room and suspected people have been talking about you. Maybe you feel as if people are avoiding you. Maybe you think people blame you for what happened. Or maybe you dread the thought that people feel sorry for you.

These kinds of feelings are common when we are going through a difficult time. But sometimes our fears about what other people are saying or doing are not true. Most people either don't know what happened or don't care.

There are, however, people who can make a bad situation even more difficult. They ask embarrassing questions about what happened. They offer unsolicited advice. They tell you stories about family members or friends who have gone through hard times. They say insensitive things in a bumbling attempt to comfort you.

Most of these people mean no harm. They probably don't even realize how inappropriate their comments or behaviors are. Chances are they won't understand until they go through a difficult time themselves. But that doesn't mean that they don't test our patience. In our frustration, we may call out to God, asking, "Why are these people acting like this?"

It may help to read the Gospel account of Martha, who complained to Jesus because of the way her sister, Mary, was acting (Luke 10:38-42). Jesus recognized that Martha was worried and distracted by many things, but Mary sat at the feet of Jesus and remained focused on the Lord. Jesus told Martha (and he tells us, too) that Mary chose the better path. When we feel stressed about what other people are saying or doing, maybe we need to turn to the Lord and sit silently in his presence. Spending some quiet time in Eucharistic Adoration may help.

One grandmother started what she called a "God Box." When she was confronted with insensitive people, she wrote their names on a piece of paper, put them into her God Box, and prayed the prayer of Jesus, "'Father, forgive them, they know not what they do'" (Luke 23:34).

What Should I Say When Other People Ask What Happened?

You don't owe anyone an explanation or an update. Only you can decide whether you trust someone enough to talk about what happened. If you don't want to share with someone, you can simply say, "I'm not ready to talk about it." If it is a legal situation, you can say, "We have been told by our attorney not to talk about it."

If you are troubled by questions or comments on social media, it's OK to block the offenders. Don't subject yourself to posts that are intrusive or insulting. Don't try to correct posts that are inaccurate. It will only spur a flurry of additional comments.

What Should I Say When People Tell Me They Want to Help?

Some people offer to help, but they don't really mean it. They feel uncomfortable and don't know what else to say. Chances are they are secretly hoping you won't respond. You can acknowledge their offer by saying, "Thanks. I will let you know if we need anything."

You may encounter people who want to help but really aren't helpful at all. They create additional problems by giving you bad advice, or they insist that you do something you don't want to do. You can tell them that you appreciate their advice and will think about it.

> A faithful friend is a sturdy shelter.
> —Sirach 6:14

There are also people who genuinely want to help and can make a big difference in a variety of ways. You can tell if they are serious by the way they offer their assistance. Do they make eye contact? Are they compassionate and sensitive to your needs? Are they trustworthy? Can you count on them to follow through with whatever they offer to do? If yes, you can respond to them by saying, "If you really want to help, I need . . ."

What Kind of Help Should I Ask For?

There are several important ways people can help:

- Some people are good listeners, and you can trust that they won't tell others what you say. They don't question you or try to change what you are thinking or feeling. They just listen, and they can be a tremendous support. You can ask for their help by saying, "I need to talk. Will you listen?"

- Some people help take your mind off what has happened. They cheer you up, make you laugh, or distract you with activities like going to a movie, out to lunch, or on a shopping trip. They may invite you to get involved in a hobby or a special project. You can ask for their help by saying, "Can you spend some time with me?"

- Some people are willing to help with household needs. They can lend a hand with garden chores, cooking, cleaning, or running errands. You can ask for their help by saying, "I need help at home."

♦ Some people can offer spiritual support for you and your family. They may suggest going to Mass together or to some parish event. You can ask for their help by saying, "I need spiritual strength. Can you guide me?

"I don't know what I would do without my close group of women friends," one grandmother admitted.

"I rely on my golfing buddies," a grandfather said. "I can talk to them about anything."

"A woman saw me crying in church, and she sat down beside me and said, 'The church is a safe place to cry,'" another grandmother recalled. "I ended up telling her everything that happened. She suggested that we meet every morning for Mass and go out for coffee afterward. I feel as if she has been a gift from God."

HOW TO HELP YOUR GRANDCHILDREN

Here are some ways to help your grandchildren deal with other people:

1. Ask your grandchildren how their friends have been helpful during this difficult time.

2. Share with your grandchildren some of your feelings about how other people react to you.

3. Explain to your grandchildren how you respond when people ask questions about what happened.

4. Talk about the help you have received from other people. Ask them what kind of help they may want or need from friends, other family members, neighbors, classmates, or teachers.

5. Assure them that you are willing to help them in any way.

PRAY ABOUT IT

Take a few moments to reflect on the powerful words of Henri Nouwen from his book *Out of Solitude.*

> When we honestly ask ourselves which persons in our lives mean the most to us, we often find that it is those who, instead of giving much advice, solutions, or cures, have chosen rather to share our pain and touch our wounds with a gentle and tender hand. The friend who can be silent with us in a moment of despair or confusion, who can stay with us in an hour of grief and bereavement, who can tolerate not knowing, not curing, and not healing, and face with us the reality of powerlessness, that is a friend who cares.[8]

QUESTIONS FOR REFLECTION AND DISCUSSION

1. What kinds of positive and negative experiences have you encountered with other people?

2. What coping mechanisms have you developed for dealing with difficult people?

3. Who are the people in your life who have helped you the most?

4. In what ways have you been able to help your grandchildren deal with other people?

---

[8] Henri J. M. Nouwen, *Out of Solitude: Three Meditations on the Christian Life* (Notre Dame, IN: Ave Maria Press, 2004), 38.

CHAPTER SIX

QUESTIONS ABOUT THE PAST

Will My Memory of What Happened Ever Fade?

Memories are like two sides of a coin, with bad memories on one side and good memories on the other side. We want to erase the bad memories of what happened. We want to stop thinking about it. We want to stop dreaming about it.

You will never completely forget the bad thing that happened, but painful memories will fade in the same way the pain of childbirth fades after the baby is born. On the other side of the coin, the good memories of people helping us through a difficult time will also begin to fade.

"I kept a journal through everything that happened," one grandmother admitted. "I recorded all of the good things as well as the bad. When I go back and read the passages, I can

It is in pardoning that we are pardoned.

—Peace Prayer, commonly attributed to St. Francis of Assisi

see how many people helped us and how God was working through everything that happened to support and console us."

Why Should I Forgive Someone Who Caused Such Destruction in Our Lives?

By choosing to forgive, you set yourself free from anger, resentment, frustration, and thoughts of retaliation. Forgiveness is good for you. It allows the poison to drain out of the wound so it can begin to heal.

If you turn to your Catholic faith, you see that in the Gospels, Jesus tells us to forgive seventy-seven times (Matthew 18:21-22). In the Lord's Prayer, Jesus tells us that God will forgive our trespasses in the same way we forgive those who trespass against us (Matthew 6:12-13; Luke 11:4). On the cross, Jesus showed us how to forgive when he prayed, "Father, forgive them, they know not what they do" (Luke 23:34).

How Can I Forgive When It Hurts So Much?

It is not easy to forgive, and forgiveness is not something that happens instantly. It begins with your willingness to forgive. Tell God that you want to forgive. Then say out loud, "I forgive this person. I am not going to hold on to anger or resentment. I forgive!"

Some people find it helpful to write their intention to forgive in a letter to God. Some people bury the letter as a sign that they are putting an end to what happened. Some people burn the letter and watch the smoke rise to God.

Praying for the person you have forgiven can help. "I pray an Our Father or Hail Mary every time I think about that person as a sign to God that I have forgiven," one grandmother explained. "Then I put it out of my mind and go on with my day."

Don't forget to pray for yourself, too, and ask God to instill in you a deep sense of peace.

What If I Can't Forget What Happened?

Forgiveness doesn't wipe the slate clean as if nothing happened. Something painful has happened, but in spite of the pain you make a conscious choice to forgive. You may dislike this person. You may never want to see this person again. This person may not want your forgiveness. This person may not deserve your forgiveness. But you choose to forgive anyway.

It may take some time before the memory of what happened and your painful feelings about it begin to subside. If negative feelings or bad memories recur, remind yourself that you have already forgiven this person. Ask God to heal that painful memory. Believe that the Lord can heal you. Believe that the Lord can make you spiritually, mentally, physically, and emotionally whole again. You can also reach out to a priest or a spiritual director if you feel as if the pain of the past weighs too heavily on you.

"I went on a men's retreat, and the priest helped us give all of our painful memories to God," one grandfather said. "The priest called it healing the pain of the past. It was very powerful."

Can You Forgive Someone Who Died?

As Catholics we believe there is a spiritual union between souls on earth, souls in purgatory, and saints in heaven. It is called the communion of saints. Because of this spiritual bond, we can pray for people who have died, and we can choose to forgive them for what happened in the past. We can also ask people who have died to forgive us for the ways we may have hurt them.

We may never know with certainty that someone who has died accepts our forgiveness or extends their forgiveness to us. But we can be at peace knowing we have attempted to forgive or to seek forgiveness. St. Ambrose assures us those who have gone before us have a level of awareness that they did not have before they died. He explains that the soul survives the body, and "being set free from the bars of the body, it sees with clear gaze those things which before, dwelling in the body, it could not see."[9]

---

9   Ambrose of Milan, *On the Death of Satyrus*, book 2, chap. 21, in Nicene and *Post-Nicene Fathers*, second series, vol. 10, ed. Philip Schaff and Henry Wace, trans. H. De Romestin (Buffalo, NY: Christian Literature Publishing Co., 1896).

How Do I Ask Someone to Forgive Me?

The first step in seeking forgiveness, whether you hurt someone intentionally or unintentionally, is to recognize that you caused this person pain. Then make a conscious decision to seek this person's forgiveness. Pray that the Holy Spirit will give you the words you need to say.

When asking for forgiveness, start by admitting to the other person that you were wrong. Don't offer explanations or excuses. Acknowledge that you have caused this person pain. Tell the person you are sorry for what happened. Then ask for forgiveness with sincerity and humility.

If the person forgives, you may feel the weight lifted. If the person refuses to forgive, be gracious enough to accept that their pain is so deep they may not be ready to let it go. Pray for that person and for yourself.

"Asking for forgiveness requires a lot of humility," one grandfather said. "It's not always easy to admit that you were wrong. But after someone forgives you, it is such a relief. You can close the door on a painful part of your life."

HOW TO HELP YOUR GRANDCHILDREN

Here are some ways to help your grandchildren deal with the past:

1. Listen as your grandchildren share good and bad memories from the past. Don't comment. Just listen.

2. Encourage your grandchildren to write down all of their good and bad memories in a journal. With younger children, you can encourage them to draw pictures.

3. Talk to them about forgiveness and how you have forgiven people who hurt you. Explain why forgiveness will take away some of their pain.

4. Admit to the times when you have had to seek forgiveness from someone you hurt.

5. Assure them that the bad memories of what happened will eventually fade and they will begin to cherish the good memories.

PRAY ABOUT IT

Set aside some time to meditate on these Scripture passages about forgiveness:

- ♦ "Therefore I tell you, whatever you ask in prayer, believe that you receive it, and you will. And whenever you stand praying, forgive, if you have anything against anyone; so that your Father also who is in heaven may forgive you your trespasses" (Mark 11:24-25).

- ♦ "For if you forgive men their trespasses, your heavenly Father also will forgive you; but if you do not forgive men their trespasses, neither will your Father forgive your trespasses" (Matthew 6:14-15).

- ♦ "Judge not, and you will not be judged; condemn not, and you will not be condemned; forgive, and you will be forgiven" (Luke 6:37).

- ♦ Put on then, as God's chosen ones, holy and beloved, compassion, kindness, lowliness, meekness, and patience, forbearing one another and, if one has a complaint against another, forgiving each other; as the Lord has forgiven you, so you also must forgive (Colossians 3:12-13).

- ♦ Let all bitterness and wrath and anger and clamor and slander be put away from you, with all malice, and be kind to one another, tenderhearted, forgiving one another, as God in Christ forgave you (Ephesians 4:31-32).

- ♦ Beloved, never avenge yourselves, but leave it to the wrath of God; for it is written, "Vengeance is mine, I will repay, says the Lord" (Romans 12:19).

QUESTIONS FOR REFLECTION AND DISCUSSION

1. How are you dealing with the mixture of good memories and bad memories?

2. In what ways have you forgiven other people?

3. In what ways have you asked for forgiveness?

4. In what ways have you helped your grandchildren deal with the past?

CHAPTER SEVEN

QUESTIONS ABOUT THE PRESENT

Who Am I Now?

In the aftermath of something bad happening, we can feel as if our lives have been completely upended. Normal routines may seem meaningless. Our lives have changed. We may begin to wonder who we are now. We may want our lives to go back to the way they were before but fear that it isn't possible. We may feel as if we are suspended between the past and the future.

At this point, we have a choice: we can become bitter, or we can become better. We can slip into despair, or we can use our feelings of loss and confusion as an invitation to explore those deep, existential questions that most people overlook in their daily lives: Who am I? Why am I here?

As you wrestle with these ultimate questions, what you believe about God, your values, and your priorities in life will come to mind. You may find that things you used to think were important take a lesser role. Things you took for granted in the past may increase in importance. New questions may arise.

At some point you will begin to see that your identity as a person was never static. Life is a journey, and you wouldn't be the same person two years from now—even if the bad thing hadn't happened.

"I am not the same as I was before my cancer diagnosis," one grandfather admitted. "Going through treatment changed me. I discovered a new sense of meaning and purpose. I developed a new appreciation for living. I felt a deeper love for my wife, my children, and my grandchildren. It changed the way I look at life."

I Used to Think of Us as the "Perfect" Family. I Can't Think of Us That Way Anymore, and It Makes Me Feel So Sad. What Should I Do?

When something bad happens, any illusions we may have had about perfection can be smashed into smithereens. But we have to ask ourselves: Was our image of a perfect family ever realistic?

The problem with the notion of a "perfect" family—whether yours or someone else's—is that it is simply not true. Every human being has faults, weaknesses, and failings. Only God is perfect.

Here are some simple ways to realign the way you think about your family after the "perfect" image has been shattered:

- **Cut the comparisons**. It is tempting to compare our family to other families, but it only leads to trouble. If we see ourselves as deficient, we stir up feelings of jealousy. If we see ourselves as superior, we fuel a false sense of pride. When we find ourselves starting to compare, we have to remind ourselves that we are all children of our heavenly Father, who has given each of us unique gifts and talents. God has also given us the grace to get through any trials and tribulations we face.

- **Check your expectations**. When our expectations for "perfection" are out of line, we open ourselves to disappointment and frustration because we can't achieve the ideal that we envision. Our unrealistic expectations set us up for failure. Letting go of expectations is not easy. Start by asking yourself, "What if I expected less?" or "What if I didn't expect anything at all?" Try to focus instead on what God is asking you to do. The Lord has promised to be with us always, and if we place our lives in his hands, we can count on him to give us the inspiration, support, and courage that we need to live according to his will.

- **Count your blessings.** One of the best ways to keep everything in perspective is to thank God for all of the good things he has bestowed on us and on our family members. We might not be perfect, and something bad may have happened, but a lot of good things have also happened, and we can count on God to continue to help us in every way!

How Can I Find God in the Present Moment?

We know from our Catholic faith that God is everywhere, but we can become so distracted that we don't recognize God's presence in our daily lives. We have to make a conscious effort to look for God in our everyday experiences.

Even when we are going through difficult times, we may feel God's presence when a stranger smiles at us. We may see God's presence in the thoughtfulness of a friend. A walk in the park or a trip to the zoo can help us to experience God in the beauty of nature. Our love for family members mirrors God's love for us. We can find God in the peacefulness of a quiet moment or in a moment of prayer.

Here are some other ways you can increase your awareness of God in the present moment:

- Look for little miracles that unfold in your daily life.

- Teach yourself to smile each time you experience God's presence.

- Help your grandchildren to recognize the presence of God in all things by sharing stories of how God touches your life.

- Make it a point to thank God—out loud or in the silence of your heart—each time his presence is revealed to you.

- Before you go to sleep, think back on the many ways you experienced God's presence during the day. Rest in the warmth of God's love.

How Can I Feel Grateful to God When So Many Bad Things Are Happening?

When times are tough and we're faced with difficulties, focusing on gratitude can be challenging. But making a conscious effort to cultivate an attitude of gratitude when facing difficulties can actually ease the burden.

"I have a 'blessings' notebook," one grandmother said. "I keep a daily log of small acts of kindness from other people, visits or calls from family members and friends, a list of good things that happen, and those special times when I feel God's presence."

Gratitude has the power to transform your life because it helps you to see yourself, other people, and any bad thing you are struggling with in a different way:

- Gratitude is an antidote to worry. Thinking about the things we're thankful for in the present moment short-stops our fear of the future.

- Gratitude is an antidote to envy. Thinking about all the things in our lives that we're grateful for dispels feelings of jealousy.

"Have patience with everyone, but especially with yourself."
—St. Francis de Sales[10]

---

[10] Jean-Pierre Camus, *The Spirit of St. Francis de Sales* (New York: Longmans, Green, and Co., 1908).

- Gratitude is an antidote to sadness. Thinking about how grateful we are for the good things in our lives helps chase the blues away.

- Gratitude is an antidote to stress. Thinking about how grateful we are for everything that is going well helps to restore a sense of peace.

- Gratitude is an antidote to taking life for granted. Thinking about the beauty of nature, the kindness of other people, and the greatness of God helps us to cultivate an attitude of gratitude in all areas of our lives.

How Can I Regain the Feeling That I Am in Control?

Most of us operate under the illusion that we are in control of our lives. Something bad happening destroys that illusion. It pushes us into a world filled with uncertainty. It forces us to accept that we are vulnerable and powerless. We can try to regain a feeling of control, but we usually find ourselves getting frustrated each time our plans are disrupted. It is much better to focus on letting go.

Let go of rigid time schedules, and allow life to unfold naturally. Stop making unnecessary demands on yourself and others. Give up on perfectionism, and recognize that everyone makes mistakes. Stop focusing on how other people should change, and instead look at how you can become a better version of yourself.

Once you begin to let go, you can redirect the energy you used to spend trying to control everything into a more positive direction. Letting go is the essence of authentic spirituality because, in the process of letting go, you allow the Holy Spirit to fill the empty spaces in your being and to lead you in new directions you may never have chosen on your own.

How Do I Know Where the Holy Spirit Is Leading Me?

The Holy Spirit is always nudging us with thoughts, ideas, inspirations, and deep longings in our hearts. As you become more aware of the presence of the Holy Spirit, you begin to notice that a new direction is unfolding. You can be sure that if you follow the promptings of the Holy Spirit, you will receive whatever help you need. Promptings from the Holy Spirit always lead toward something that is life-giving for you and for other people.

As you become more experienced in recognizing the movement of the Holy Spirit in your life, you will begin to recognize changes in yourself. You may find yourself becoming more understanding—not just of others, but also of yourself. You may find yourself becoming more compassionate toward other people. You may find yourself becoming more patient with whatever is happening. You may find yourself becoming less self-centered. You may feel a deep sense of peace.

How Can the Holy Spirit Work Through Me to Help My Children and Grandchildren?

Pray. Ask the Holy Spirit to guide you in all of your interactions with your children and grandchildren. Ask the Holy Spirit to allow God's love to flow through you to touch them. Begin to envision yourself as a channel through which God's love can constantly pour out.

A powerful prayer you can use is the Prayer of the Loving Look.[11] There are no words. You simply imagine that God's love is pouring out from you as you gaze at another person. You don't have to limit this prayer to family members. You can share the Prayer of the Loving Look with everyone you meet.

"Loving God and loving others is the essence of what life is all about," one grandmother explained. "I try to love my grandchildren unconditionally as God loves me unconditionally. I try to be accepting, nonjudgmental, and understanding. I try to pass on to them—not so much with words, but with my actions—that the foundation for my life is my Catholic faith. I tell them that God gives us special gifts and talents. I help them recognize their gifts, and I encourage them to use their gifts and talents in ways that will make the world a better place. I take every opportunity to help them see the presence of God in my life and in their lives."

---

[11] See Vinita Hampton Wright, "A Long, Loving Look at the Real," Ignatian Spirituality, https://www.ignatianspirituality.com/a-long-loving-look-at-the-real/.

HOW TO HELP YOUR GRANDCHILDREN

Here are some ways you can help your grandchildren through difficult times:

1. Ask your grandchildren if they want to come out of this experience bitter or better. Share with them how you emerged better after bad things that happened in the past.

2. Talk about what lessons can be learned from this. Help them to grow from what happened.

3. Encourage your grandchildren not to compare themselves with other people because everybody has faults, failings, and bad things that happen in their lives. Comparisons are useless and only make us feel worse.

4. Share the ways you recognize the presence of God in midst of this crisis. Talk about how God gives you strength and a sense of direction.

5. Engage your grandchildren in making a list of all the things they are grateful for in your lives. Thank God with them for all of the good things.

6. Invite your grandchildren to pray with you to the Holy Spirit for comfort, guidance, understanding, wisdom, and love.

PRAY ABOUT IT

Take some time to reflect on this powerful prayer from St. Teresa of Ávila:

> Lord, grant that I may always allow
> myself to be guided by you,
>
> always follow your plans and perfectly
> accomplish your holy will.
>
> Grant that in all things, great and small,
> today and all the days of my life,
>
> I may do whatever you require of me.
>
> Help me respond to the slightest prompting of your grace,
>
> so that I may be your trustworthy instrument for your honor.
>
> May your will be done in time and in eternity
> by me, in me, and through me.[12]

QUESTIONS FOR REFLECTION AND DISCUSSION

1. How has your sense of who you are changed during this difficult time?

2. In what ways have you had to "let go" of unrealistic expectations?

3. How have you experienced God's presence?

4. In what ways have you helped your grandchildren in the present moment?

---

[12] Commonly attributed to St. Teresa of Ávila.

CHAPTER EIGHT

QUESTIONS ABOUT THE FUTURE

How Can I Believe Something Good Will Come Out of This?

When bad things happen, we often wonder if something good can happen again. St. Paul assures us that "all things work for good for those who love God" (Romans 8:28). That doesn't mean whatever bad thing that happened was good. It does mean that good things can happen in the aftermath of bad things.

Family bonds may get stronger. You may find new ways of doing things. You may meet new people and develop new friendships. You may decide to create public awareness or lobby for legislation that will prevent the same bad thing from happening to someone else. You may get involved in a prayer group or support group. You may decide to volunteer or to raise money to help others who are struggling. You may learn new lessons. In time, you may begin to see a bigger picture that gives new meaning and purpose to your life.

What New Lessons Can I Learn from This?

The biggest lesson you can learn from something bad happening is that you can rely on God to help you through difficult times. With God's help, you can bear the pain. With God's help, you can walk through difficulties moment by moment. With God's help, you can emerge from this a better person than before.

You can gain understanding—not just of others, but also of yourself and your situation.

You can gain empathy and compassion for other people who suffer.

You can grow in love and recognize that the essence of life is our ability to love God and love our neighbor.

You can grow in wisdom as you begin to see the world as God sees it.

"I've learned that every person is important," one grandfather said. "Every person should be treated with respect and dignity."

"I've learned that I can't judge other people," a grandmother admitted. "I don't know what is going on in another person's life."

"I've learned what is truly meaningful in life," another grandfather said. "It is the importance of family and the deepening of faith."

Will I Ever Be at Peace?

Yes. When we turn to God during difficult times, we will receive the gift of peace in the depths of ourselves. We may still experience turmoil on the surface of our lives, but deep inside us the gift of peace eases our fears and helps us to remain calm.

Jesus promised us the gift of peace when he said, "Peace I leave with you; my peace I give to you; not as the world gives do I give to you" (John 14:27).

It is the same peace that St. Paul says "surpasses all understanding" and will keep our hearts and minds in Christ Jesus (Philippians 4:7). If we place our trust in God, we can rely on this gift of inner peace to sustain us no matter what happens.

"My life did not turn out like a fairy tale where people live happily ever after," one grandparent admitted. "But I can say that after a series of bad things happening, it is possible to live peacefully ever after. It is this deep sense of inner peace that sustains me."

> "Trust the past to God's mercy, the present to God's love, the future to God's providence."
>
> —St. Augustine of Hippo[13]

---

[13] Commonly attributed to St. Augustine of Hippo.

Will Our Lives Ever Go Back to Normal?

Your life will never go back to exactly the way it was before something bad happened. Life has changed. You have suffered. You have grown in ways you never expected. You have learned new ways of coping. You have adapted.

You have embarked on a new way of living your life in spite of the pain you suffered and the losses you incurred. You have turned a corner, and you are moving in a new direction. Some people call it "the new normal."

How Will I Know When the "New Normal" Begins?

Your "new normal" is already unfolding. Here are some signs you are entering into a new normal:

- You laugh more often.
- You worry less.
- You feel more energetic.
- You feel hopeful.
- You feel grateful for little things that happen.
- You welcome new people into your life.
- You look forward to the future.
- You accept that life will go on—not in the way it had been before but in a way that has meaning and purpose.

HOW TO HELP YOUR GRANDCHILDREN

Here are some ways to help your grandchildren as they look to the future:

1. Help them to understand something good will come. Things may not be the same as they were before, but their lives can move in a positive direction.

2. Talk to your grandchildren about the new things they have learned from what happened. Help them to find ways to use their bad experiences to help other people who are struggling through similar difficulties.

3. Explain to your grandchildren that while things will never go back to exactly the way they were before, their lives will settle down.

4. Talk about the "new normal" and how their lives will move in a new direction.

5. Assure them that whatever bad thing happened in the past will not necessarily recur. If other bad things happen, they will receive the strength and courage to deal with them. Promise that you will always be there for them.

PRAY ABOUT IT

Take some time to reflect on this passage from Thomas Merton's *Thoughts in Solitude*:

> My Lord and God, I have no idea where I am going. I do not see the road ahead of me. I cannot know for certain where it will end. Nor do I really know myself, and the fact that I think that I am following your will does not mean that I am actually doing so. But I believe that the desire to please you does in fact please you. And I hope that I have that desire in all that I am doing. I hope that I will never do anything apart from that desire. And I know that if I do this you will lead me by the right road though I may know nothing about it.[14]

QUESTIONS FOR REFLECTION AND DISCUSSION

1. What are some of the good things that have happened?
2. What lessons are you learning?
3. In what ways are you growing into your "new normal"?
4. In what ways have you helped your grandchildren move into the future?

---

14 Thomas Merton, *Thoughts in Solitude* (New York: Farrar, Straus and Giroux, 1956), 79.

AFTERWORD

My fifteen-year-old grandson and I like to try different restaurants for Sunday brunch. The food is great, but even better is the chance to talk about what is happening in our lives. One Sunday morning I told him I was working on this book for grandparents about what to do when bad things happen.

I knew it would spark his interest. During the past year, he dealt with several medical issues, while also navigating the challenging transition from eighth grade to high school. A few months later, an electrical fire at his house destroyed almost everything he owned. The house was a complete loss, and his family moved into temporary housing until a new house could be built.

"What advice would you offer grandparents on how to help grandkids during difficult times?" I asked.

He paused for several minutes. I resisted the temptation to interrupt the silence because I could see that he was deep in thought. Then he said there are three things grandparents can do.

1. "You can help us make good decisions."

He explained that, when something bad happens, kids have to make decisions. I pointed out that he would hate it if I told him what to do. He agreed, but he explained that helping with decisions is different than saying to do this or do that.

"Grandparents have been through a lot in their lives, so they have wisdom," he said. "They can help us with good judgment."

I asked him to explain good judgment. He said good judgment is figuring out which path to pick when there are several ways to go. Good judgment is deciding what to think and what to say as well as what to do.

"How do grandparents do that?" I asked.

I was surprised when he told me that I do it all the time by listening as he talks about decisions he has to make and by asking questions that make him think. Then he can decide what is the best thing to do.

"OK," I said. "What is the second thing grandparents can do to help grandkids when bad things happen?"

2. "You can help us learn from our mistakes."

He smiled when he said, "I like it when you tell stories about mistakes you made when you were young. You always tell me mistakes can be a learning process if you change your life for the better after you make a mistake!"

Then he reminded me of a story I told him about trying to steer my bicycle with my feet when I was seven years old. I fell and broke my arm.

"That was a mistake," he laughed. "But you learned from it, and I learned from it because you told me the story."

He went on to say that when he makes a mistake, I never make him feel bad about it. That's why he is never afraid to tell me when something bad happens. He said he knows I won't judge him or blame him or be angry with him.

"OK," I said. "What's the third thing grandparents can do?"

3. "You can help us deal with our emotions."

We talked about emotions that arise when bad things happen—fear, anger, frustration, sadness, guilt, shame, resentment, and depression.

"Feelings are complicated," he said. "Sometimes you can have bad feelings and good feelings at the same time, like at funerals when people are sad, but they also tell stories that make everyone laugh."

I asked what grandparents can do to help grandchildren deal with emotions.

"Grandparents understand how we are feeling because they probably felt the same way at some time in their lives," he said. "Grandparents know that you can't automatically stop feeling a certain way. Grandparents can let you go with the flow of feelings. They can listen and let us know they understand."

He also suggested grandparents can remind grandkids that bad feelings eventually end and good feelings will come back again.

Why Bad Things Happen

I asked my grandson if it helps when grandparents pray for their grandchildren. He said yes, but he admitted that he struggles with why an all-powerful God allows bad things to happen.

"I know God gave us free will and people can choose to do bad things," he said. "I know illnesses and natural disasters can happen."

He also said he understands accidents like the faulty wiring that caused his house to burn. He does not understand why some people are miraculously saved and others are left to suffer.

"Not even the wisest grandparent could answer that question," I told him. "It is one of the great mysteries of life. But if we turn to our Catholic faith, we can see that sometimes God allows bad things to happen so something good can come from it. God did not stop the crucifixion of Jesus, but the suffering and death of Jesus led to resurrection and new life on Easter Sunday."

AFTERWORD

God Is Always with Us

There was a moment of silence. Then my grandson admitted he was angry at God for allowing bad things to happen to him.

"It's OK to tell God that you are angry," I told him. "It is one of the best forms of prayer because it comes from the deepest part of yourself. God will not get angry at you for being angry. God loves you no matter how you feel."

I explained that God never promised us a life without pain or suffering. God did promise to be with us always—through all the good times and all the bad times.

We talked about when I was diagnosed with breast cancer several years ago.

"I learned from that difficult time that I could choose to believe breast cancer was a curse, or I could believe that in some strange way breast cancer would lead to a blessing. If I believed breast cancer was a curse, it would take me down a dark path toward self-pity and depression. By believing that something good would come from it, I could cling to the hope that God would carry me through it and transform my life for the better."

He admitted that he had been afraid I would die when I was diagnosed with cancer. I assured him that I am OK.

"God still has things for me to do in this world," I told him. "And God has things for you to do with your life."

The conversation paused as we finished our food, but I was curious about what he was thinking.

"Did I sound too preachy?" I asked.

He shook his head no. He said he just needed to think about it.

I knew our time together was coming to an end when the waitress brought the check. "Is there anything else grandparents can do?" I asked.

His eyes twinkled and he smiled. "Yes," he said. "You can teach us how much money to leave for a tip!"

theWORD among us®

The Word Among Us publishes a monthly devotional magazine, books, Bible studies, and pamphlets that help Catholics grow in their faith.

To learn more about who we are and what we publish, visit www.wau.org. There you will find a variety of Catholic resources that will help you grow in your faith.

Your review makes a difference! If you enjoyed this book, please consider sharing your review on Amazon using the QR code below.

Embrace His Word
Listen to God . . .

www.wau.org